DK

2/13

FACTS AT YOUR FINGERTIPS

INVENTION AND TECHNOLOGY

BUILDINGS AND STRUCTURES

BOOKS

Published by Brown Bear Books Ltd

4877 N. Circulo Bujia
Tucson, AZ 85718
USA

and

First Floor
9-17 St. Albans Place
London N1 0NX

© 2012 Brown Bear Books Ltd

Library of Congress Cataloging-in-Publication Data

Jackson, Tom, 1972-
  Buildings and structures.
        p. cm. – (Facts at your fingertips
                invention and technology)
  Includes index.
  ISBN 978-1-936333-41-7 (library binding)
1.   Structural engineering–Juvenile literature. 2.   Building–
Juvenile literature. 3.   Buildings–Juvenile literature.   I. Title.

  TA634.J33 2011
  690–dc23
                                        2011046991

Editorial Director: Lindsey Lowe
Editor: Tom Jackson
Creative Director: Jeni Child
Designer: Lynne Lennon
Children's Publisher: Anne O'Daly
Production Director: Alastair Gourlay

Printed in the United States of America

Picture Credits

Front Cover: Shutterstock, kasia
Back Cover: Shutterstock, Carlos Neto

Alamy: Qapphotos 48b; **istockphoto:** 17t; **Public Domain:** Averette 27t; Roman Bonnefoy/romanceor 14t; David Iliff 36-37; **Shutterstock:** 4; Asianet-Pakistan 32; Achim Baque 8b; Stephane Bidouze 35b, 61t; Bocky 58bl; Dubassy 22t; Helen & vlad Filatov 33t; Jean Frooms 19b; hainaul Hoto 18; Alison Hancock 28b; Patricia Hofmeester 57b; Alexander Ishchenko 17b; Attila Jandi 6b; Emin Kuliyev 20b, 60; Jon Le Bon 43t; Leungchopan 14b; Liza 41; Wade H. Massie 35t; Vladmir Melnik 20t; Dudarev Mikhail 9; Mundoview 12t; Carlos Neto 1; Olson Tyler 7; Qapphotos.com 27b; Howard Sandler 6t; Richard Semik 45b; Serg 34b; Floris Slooff 36; Tupungato 11br; Zuanlu Wang 27b; Lawrence Wee 24b; Gareth Weeks 42; Gary Yim 26; Andrey Yurlov 19t; **Thinkstock:** Ablestock 30b, 40b; Comstock 50; Digital Vision 10t; Hemera 8t, 12b, 22b, 48t, 56, 57t; istockphoto 3, 5b, 10b, 16, 25t, 29, 30-31, 31br, 38, 40, 44, 51b, 53, 58br; Photodisc 24t, 40-41; Photos.com 5t, 11bl, 34t, 46, 47, 51t, 52t, 54, 58t, 62; **Topfoto:** Topham Picturepoint 45t

Brown Bear Books has made every attempt to contact the copyright holder. If you have any information please email smortimer@windmillbooks.co.uk

All artwork copyright Brown Bear Books Ltd

CONTENTS

TRADITIONAL STRUCTURES

Since the dawn of history people have constructed their buildings from the materials available to them in their local environment, and until the invention of engines 200 years ago, building materials were made and lifted using muscle power alone.

Nowadays most buildings are made from bricks, steel, and concrete, with glass windows and shingled roofs. However, in the earliest days of humanity people built temporary dwellings out of easily available materials such as grass, mud, and sticks, using very primitive tools. In many places the earliest humans lived in caves and therefore didn't have to build shelters at all, while herders simply lived under the open sky.

Many ancient peoples had no fixed homes. Instead, they would travel from place to place, moving either when the seasons changed or when they needed fresh pastures for their herds. These people were called nomads. Many of these tribes lived in tents, which they dismantled and took with them whenever they moved. Nomadic societies still exist on many continents.

There is a theory that the continent of America was first populated by people who walked across the Bering Strait (which separates

▼ *Traditional building techniques worked very well, and many old buildings still stand, such as St. Paul's Cathedral in London, which was completed in 1710. In 2000, a new bridge was built to connect the south of the city to the cathedral. However, it took engineers nearly two years more to stop the high-tech suspension bridge from wobbling.*

▲ *The tents used by many Native American groups are called tipis. The rawhide tents had holes at the top to allow fire smoke to escape from inside.*

Asia from Alaska) when a land bridge emerged there during the last Ice Age. This is evident not only in the genetic characteristics of the Native people but also in comparisons of their dwellings. The typical dwelling of many Asian peoples, called a *yurt*, *jirga*, or *ger*, is similar to a type of tent used by some Native Americans.

Gradually people settled and adapted to their environment. As a result, the wooden frames that formed the basis of their buildings became more robust, and the animal hides and woven fabrics that had previously been used as coverings were replaced by sturdier, heavier materials such as wood, grass, and mud. This change gave the structures a new strength and durability. Eventually, the wooden frameworks would become stronger and stronger as the dwellings grew in size.

SOCIETY AND INVENTIONS

Mobile homes

While some nomadic people traditionally built new shelters wherever they went from local materials, other groups took their homes with them. The shelters of these people had to be reliable, weatherproof, mobile, and versatile. In order to meet these needs, a variety of basic tent designs were created.

Some of these styles have not changed for many hundreds of years. The Bedouin people of the Middle East and North Africa, for example, live in the same style of tent as their ancestors. Their tents are made from woven cloth that is pulled tight over poles, with only one wall and a roof to protect the occupants from the wind. The Mongolian *ger* (or *yurt*, below), on the other hand, is more like a portable house than a tent. The walls are made from criss-crossed fences, while poles stretching over the top form the roof. This frame is then covered by a thick blanket of felt that keeps the heat of the fire inside the home.

▲ *Everything needed to make a family's* ger—*and the beds and furniture inside—are transported on dozens of camels, yaks, and horses. Everything can be packed away into tight bundles—except the ger's solid wooden front door.*

Building materials of the world

In different parts of the world people had different materials available to them. To a great extent this defined the type of buildings that they constructed. In the marshes of southern Iraq, for example, reed rushes and mud from the wetlands were used to make long pillars that were inserted into holes dug in the ground in two parallel lines. The tops of the pillars were then bent over and fastened together with the opposite pillar, making a row of arches. These arches were attached together by thin bundles of reeds, and reed matting then covered the entire building. These techniques are 6,000 years old and are still used today.

In places such as Scandinavia, the Swiss Alps, and the Himalayas, where timber has

▶ *This longhouse made by the Native American people of eastern Canada has a frame of wood and was covered in skins in cold weather. The building could house 20 families.*

MORE THAN MUD HUTS

Mud has been used for building all over the world. Mud was used by the Pueblo people of North America as well as in Mali, West Africa, where many mud buildings still stand. Made well, mud houses can be sturdy and also very beautiful. The great ziggurats (raised platforms) of ancient Mesopotamia were made from mud bricks. Despite being about 4,000 years old, the ruins of these mud constructions can still be seen.

▲ *The Great Mosque at Djenne, in Mali, West Africa, is made of mud and wood and is nearly 800 years old, although it has been rebuilt several times.*

THE IGLOO

The Inuits, who live in the Arctic, still use snow to make temporary shelters, called igloos, in the same way they have for centuries. Igloos are made from huge blocks of frozen snow and are formed in the shape of a dome, a design that offers great natural strength. Loose snow is then packed over the top, filling in gaps. When the dome has been made, the builder goes inside, tightly sealing the igloo from the cold air outside. A lamp is then lit. The hot air, having no way to escape, begins to melt the blocks of snow. Then, when cold air is allowed in again, the melted snow quickly freezes. This process cements together the blocks and forms a smooth surface of ice on the inside of the igloo. The structure may be further strengthened by sleet, which freezes as it runs down the sides of the building. Igloos can be linked to one another via roofed passages, forming community dwellings of between three and five rooms capable of housing 15 to 20 people.

▲ Igloos are not used as permanent housing, just as temporary shelters while Inuit people are hunting for seals far from home in the summer. Blocks of clear ice are fitted between the slabs of white snow to make windows.

generally been plentiful, people have tended to make their houses from wood. Tall, straight-trunked trees such as pine, fir, and beech are particularly suited to this use. The log cabins of these areas are often made by flattening two sides of the long trunks and cutting the ends so that they fit together. Houses are still often built completely out of timber today.

Building in stone

Buildings constructed from stone are strong because it is such a hard and durable material. Some of the earliest stone buildings date back as far as 2770 B.C.—that means they have survived for almost 5,000 years. One civilization

WATTLE AND DAUB

One of the oldest building materials is wattle and daub. This material has been found in some of the oldest settlements know, such as Çatalhöyük, a 9,000-year-old ruined city in central Turkey. Wattle and daub is a composite material, making use of two very different substances to create a sturdy structure. The wattle is a fence made by weaving thin branches around timber supports. This inner structure is then filled in and covered by the daub, a soft material made of whatever is available—mud, straw, horsehair, and even dung.

that used stone to spectacular effect was that of ancient Egypt. In order to extract the stone from the quarry, the Egyptians used pickaxes to chip away at the rock until five sides of a rectangular block were exposed. They then drilled holes along the sixth face and filled them with wooden wedges. Doused with water, the wedges would expand, breaking the block from the stone face. The masons then used mallets and chisels to shape the block into a smooth rectangle, checking their work with straight edges, set squares, and plummets (pieces of lead attached to a line used to check the alignment of vertical surfaces). Such simple tools remained in use right up until the Industrial Revolution.

▲ The Lycian people cut tombs out of the rocky cliffs of western Turkey about 2,400 years ago.

INCA WALL

The Incas of South America built very strong stone walls (below, in Cuzco, Peru). The walls were dry—the stones were not glued together with cement. Instead, each stone was cut to fit together so exactly that you could not fit a knife blade between them. This was all the more amazing since the Incas only had cutting tools made from soft metals, such as bronze and gold, and stone axes.

Temples and tombs

Because it was quite costly to quarry and maneuver, stone was mainly used for state or royal buildings. The most famous ancient structure made from stone is the Great Pyramid of the pharaoh Cheops (or Khufu) at Giza, Egypt. Built over 4,000 years ago, it reached an incredible height of 481 ft (147 m), 172 ft

(54 m) taller than the Statue of Liberty. Similar pyramids can be seen in Central America. They were built from around 900 B.C. by such civilizations as the Olmecs, Toltecs, and Mayans. Many of these temples have been found in the middle of thick rain forests. Like their Egyptian counterparts, the builders of these incredible structures carried out their tasks using the most basic of tools.

Ancient Greek stonemasons were also highly skilled. Greek builders fitted blocks of stone together on site after trimming them to slot into one another. Any gaps between the stones would be filled with smaller pieces.

HOW THE GREAT PYRAMID WAS MADE

The main stone used for the construction of the pyramids at Giza was limestone, with the more beautiful granite used to provide a finishing layer. Limestone was readily available locally, but the nearest site from which granite could be quarried was Aswan, about 800 miles (1,300 km) away. Archaeologists are unsure as to how the stone was carried so far. One theory suggests that it could have been brought along the Nile River in barges. The barges probably brought the stone as near as possible, and then from that stage, teams of people and animals moved the huge stone blocks small distances at a time, eventually reaching the building site.

The next question is how these huge weights were transported to the top of the pyramid. Historians believe that the Egyptian builders used a ramp, made from rubble, sand, or broken mud brick, up which the stones were pushed using human and animal power. The angle of the ramp could not have been more than 10 degrees, since if it was any steeper than this, humans and animals would not have been strong enough to get the stones up the slope. Historians think that the ramp leading to the top of the Great Pyramid (right) was constructed like a spiral, wrapping itself around the pyramid, and was taken down after the last stone was laid.

In Africa the ancient walled city of Great Zimbabwe was built from stone between around A.D. 1200 and 1450. In its heyday it housed a population of nearly 20,000. The inhabitants of Great Zimbabwe, which spread over an area of 60 acres (24 hectares), lived in thatched huts built from a mixture of clay and granite gravel. By looking at the remains of the walls of this city, it is possible to see how the builders learned how to build dry stone walls taller and stronger. The earlier walls are built unevenly, with different shaped blocks of stone, whereas the later stonework has a better finish, with uniform size and shape.

Arguably, the ancient world's most impressive stone structure is the Great Wall of China. Giving an exact date to the structure's origins is difficult, but the first attempts to build

USING CONCRETE

In order to glue the bricks of their buildings into place, the Romans used a mortar composed of sand, lime, and water. However, sometime in the 2nd century B.C. they added a new ingredient into the mixture. This was *pulvis puteoli*, or *pozzolana*, a kind of ash that was found on the slopes of Mount Vesuvius, a volcano near Naples, Italy. When added to the mortar, this produced concrete, a material that became both very strong and highly durable when dry. In fact, concrete was so strong that the Romans soon began to use it to form the interior of walls, using the brickwork simply as an outer shell. Eventually, some buildings were made entirely of concrete. The wet concrete was poured into a wooden framework that was removed as soon as the concrete had hardened. After the fall of the Roman Empire the technique of making concrete was lost for many centuries. It was revived in Britain in the 18th century. Portland cement—a high-quality concrete extracted from quarries on Britain's south coast—was patented by the engineer Joseph Aspdin (1778–1855) in 1824.

▲ Concrete slabs and walls are made by pouring the liquid mixture into wooden structures called forms. The concrete is smoothed over and allowed to dry into a hard solid before the wooden form is taken down.

▲ The Pantheon in Rome was made from concrete in A.D. 126. The building's 42-foot (43.3 m) dome is the largest dome ever built from non-reinforced concrete.

a unified wall date back to the 3rd century B.C. In the east, the core of the wall was built up from rubble and covered with an outer skin of stone. In this part of China stone was readily available. In the west, where stone was hard to find, the wall was made up of a mixture of local soil and water. This was packed between two wooden barriers and then left to dry hard.

Bricks and concrete

Bricks have been used for thousands of years. The earliest Greek temples were made from mud bricks and had thatched roofs. Also, some of the earlier and simpler Egyptian tombs were made

▼ As this close up of the Colosseum, the great arena in Rome, shows, Roman buildings were constructed of bricks and then covered by slabs of stone.

▲ The Great Wall of China is 4,112 miles (6,168 km) of walls and trenches that connect natural features such as hills and rivers into a barrier stretching across China.

from mud bricks. Because they are held together with clay, which is found in most soils, bricks were available almost anywhere. They were also easier and more economical to use than stone.

The clay or mud would be molded into a brick shape and left to dry in the sun. People later discovered that if bricks were heated in a kiln (oven) to a greater temperature, they would be stronger and more durable. The size and shape of bricks also improved. Initially, bricks were modeled by hand into the shape of a loaf of bread, until builders discovered that it was easier to use a mold to make them into smaller,

▲ *Mud bricks are laid out to dry in the sunshine, becoming rock-hard after several days.*

neater shapes that could be cooked more efficiently in the kiln.

Whereas the Byzantine and later European builders used brick itself as a decorative surface, the Romans usually covered, or faced, their brick buildings with stone, marble, or more frequently with concrete. Strong and versatile, concrete had a huge influence on Roman architecture.

The arch, the vault, and the dome

A major development that allowed stone to be used to span large areas was the arch. Although the Egyptians and the Greeks had both used the arch, it was the Romans who were responsible for its true development. Whereas the Greeks reveled in the marvel of their columns, the Romans' use of the arch made it possible for them to cover large spans using stone or concrete without the limitation of columns and flat beams.

THE POST-AND-LINTEL SYSTEM

One of the oldest and simplest means of constructing buildings is the post-and-lintel system. It uses a lintel, or beam, rested on a set of two posts, or columns, that are set into holes in the ground, or foundations. One of the best known post-and-lintel constructions is Stonehenge (below), a 4,000-year-old giant stone circle that was built on a high plain in southwest England. The post-and-lintel system was further developed by the ancient Greeks, who used elaborately designed columns to support their temples.

The system has its limitations. The material used in the lintels has to be strong when placed under tension (when stretched), while that used in the posts has to be strong under compression. Stone, the most durable material available to ancient builders, cracks under tension. Therefore stone lintels spanning long distances would collapse.

Cranes

The first mention of the use of cranes comes in the work of the Roman architect Vitruvius, who wrote an instruction manual for builders in the first century B.C. The cranes of Vitruvius's day tended to be very basic affairs, consisting simply of a long pole with a pulley on the end of it. The pole was held in place by guy ropes. At one end of the main rope was a winch. Between them the pulley and the winch allowed large weights to be hoisted with comparatively little human effort. The Roman device was improved in the 15th century when the derrick crane (below) was developed by the architects of Renaissance Italy. The pulley was at the end of a movable arm known as a jib. This made the crane a far more flexible and effective machine. In some cases the crane would be powered by a treadmill. Cranes powered by steam engines arrived in 1805, thanks to the efforts of Scottish engineer John Rennie (1761–1821). Hydraulic power came 41 years later when the British arms manufacturer William Armstrong (1810–1900) converted a steam-powered crane to use at Newcastle docks.

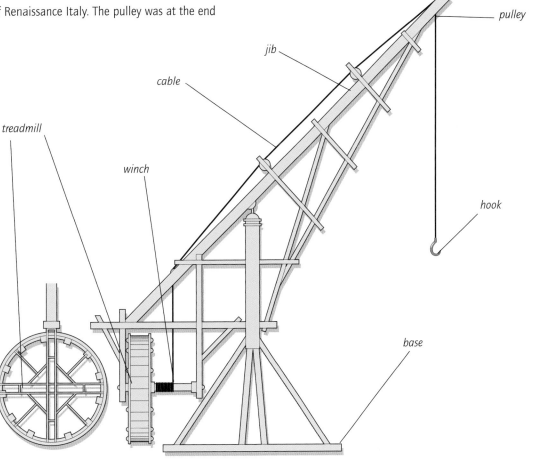

One of the most impressive surviving Roman arches is the aqueduct at the Pont du Gard in Nîmes, present-day France. Built over 2,000 years ago, the Pont du Gard is made up of three tiers of arches. The Colosseum in Rome, Italy, is another awe-inspiring example of the use of the arch. Constructed in around A.D. 75, this amphitheater consisted of four tiers. The first three tiers were made up of individual arches, which illustrates the way that the Romans used the arch to support the weight of tall buildings.

The principles behind the arch extend to the vault. A vault is basically an arch that has been

◄ The Church of Saint-Séverin in Paris has a high-vaulted ceiling held up by stone ribs that spread out from the wall columns.

lengthened to form a tunnel. The vault can cover far greater amounts of space than traditional post-and-lintel structures. It was used in Mesopotamia (modern-day Iraq) as early as 700 B.C. and was further developed by the Romans. However, these simple barrel vaults either needed substantial buttressing or very thick walls to support their weight. The problem was overcome partially in the first century B.C. with the introduction of the groin vault. Vaults were made to cross at right

SCAFFOLDING

▲ *Modern scaffold is made from steel poles, locked together by clamps. In Asia, wooden scaffolds are sometimes used even for tall buildings.*

While ancient Egyptian builders worked on tall buildings from specially constructed ramps, their Roman counterparts used scaffolding. This was a wooden framework constructed around the building from which the workmen could carry out their tasks. While we know little of the exact nature of Roman scaffolding, it is likely that it closely resembled that used in medieval Europe. This was made up of wooden poles lashed together with hemp ropes. The taller the structure, the thicker the poles. Platforms were made out of wicker, although these were replaced by wooden planks when heavy mechanical saws were introduced in the 15th century.

SCIENTIFIC PRINCIPLES

The arch

The arch is an ingenious design based on mathematical principles. Arches work because the wedge-shaped blocks (*voussoirs*) that form the round arch push the weight from above them down and out to the sides of the opening, allowing the weight to be carried by the two supporting posts (imposts). However, the force is not simply directed vertically downward: there is also a side thrust, so abutments are needed to stop the feet of the arch moving outward. Because an arch cannot support itself during its construction, it needs to be built onto a temporary support. The temporary support, known as centering, is usually made of timber and is itself supported from underneath. The *voussoirs* are laid at either end on to the imposts and are built up until they almost meet in the middle, at which point the keystone is laid. The keystone is the central *voussoir* that holds the whole arch together.

In the 12th century, European architects discovered that the Roman semicircle (1) was not the most efficient form of arch. They found that the greater the height (or rise) of the arch as opposed to its span, the less side-thrust was exerted at its base. This discovery led to the Gothic arches (2) that dominated the churches of medieval Europe.

1. Roman semicircular arch

2. Gothic arch

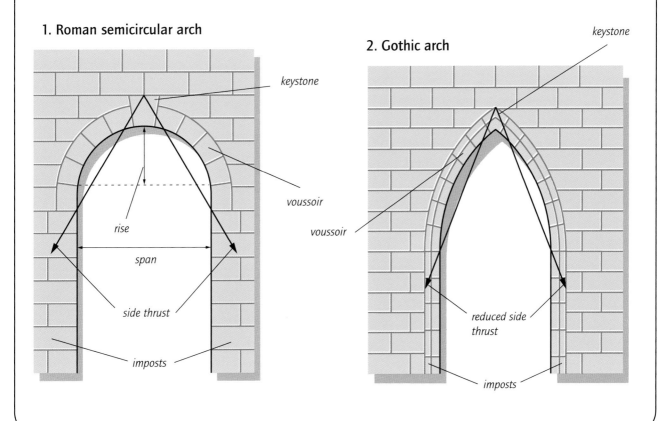

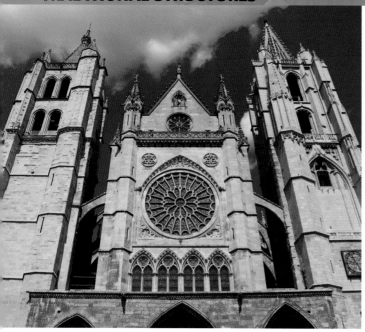

◀ The tall towers of the cathedral at León in Spain are connected by buttresses to provide extra support.

The dome of St. Paul's Cathedral, built by the English architect Christopher Wren (1632–1723) and completed in 1710, is embraced by chains for the same reason.

Generally, however, the world saw surprisingly few advances in building techniques between the fall of the Roman Empire and the Industrial Revolution some 1,300 years later, when the discovery of new methods of making iron and steel would revolutionize the building industry. Even as late as the 18th century most of the techniques used by the world's builders would have been familiar to their ancestors who lived hundreds, and in some instances thousands, of years earlier.

angles, and the edge formed at the point where the vaults crossed was known as the groin.

Heavy buttressing at the intersection allowed thinner walls to be used. The art of the vault developed slowly over the centuries and eventually reached its high point in the Gothic cathedrals of 16th-century Europe, when highly complex systems of interlocking vaults, arches, and flying buttresses (half-arches used as supports) were used to spectacular effect.

Another Roman structure that enjoyed a revival in medieval Europe was the dome. In principle the dome worked like a circular arch. Because of the weight involved, the supporting walls had to be very thick to counteract the problem of side-thrust. For example, the Pantheon, Greece, built in the 2nd century A.D., needed walls 20 ft (6 m) thick to support its 142-ft (45 m) span. In 1432 the Italian architect Filippo Brunelleschi (1377–1446) attempted to overcome the problem by placing ribs around the base of the dome of Florence's cathedral.

FACTS AND FIGURES

● The main section of the Great Wall of China is over 2,000 miles (3,200 km) long. The oldest section dates to at least 220 B.C.

● The oldest tent ever found is thought to be over 40,000 years old. It was discovered in Russia. Mammoth bones were used as the supports, and the skin of the mammoth was probably used as covering.

● The world's largest igloo is the Ice Hotel in Jukkasjärvi, Sweden. Rebuilt every year, the complex covers an area of 4,500 square yards (3,500 sq. m) and includes a church and a movie theater.

● The 481-ft (147 m) tall Great Pyramid at Giza, Egypt, contains approximately 2 million stones. They weigh an average of 2.5 tons (2.3 metric tons) each.

SOCIETY AND INVENTIONS

Chimneys

Although the Romans developed relatively sophisticated methods of heating buildings—most notably the use of hot-air channels concealed in walls and floors—these techniques were lost with the collapse of the empire. In early medieval Europe most buildings were heated simply by a central fire, and were often based around large, communal, heated rooms. The smoke from the fire escaped through a hole in the roof. This was not a very satisfactory arrangement: the hole let in wind and rain, while much of the smoke stayed in the room. These problems were solved by the arrival of the brick fireplace and chimney sometime between the 12th and 14th centuries. Most of the smoke from the hearth was channeled up the chimney and out into the open air. The invention had a fairly major social effect, allowing smaller rooms to be heated, and thus causing a shift away from the communal lifestyle of old.

▲ *Hampton Court Palace, built by England's Henry VIII 500 years ago, has 241 chimneys.*

▼ *The Dome of the Rock in Jerusalem was built in the 7th century. The dome is semicircular and constructed of wood.*

MODERN BUILDINGS

People have lived in cities since the ancient civilizations of Egypt and Mesopotamia, but only in the last 200 years have cities grown to the size and density we know today—and our buildings have also grown to match.

The change from an agricultural society to a mainly industrial one is known as the Industrial Revolution. It started first in Britain, around 1750, and spread rapidly to the United States. By the 1850s much of the Western world had become industrialized but the same process is still taking place in other parts of the world.

It was the Industrial Revolution that first prompted the large-scale migration of people to

▲ Burj Khalifa, in Dubai, is the tallest building in the world. Completed in 2009, it reaches 2,717 ft (828 m) into the sky and has 160 floors.

LONDON'S CRYSTAL PALACE

Constructed to the design of the botanist and gardener Sir Joseph Paxton (1801-1865), the Crystal Palace was effectively a gigantic iron and glass greenhouse that was built for London's Great Exhibition of 1851. This huge structure—1,848 ft (563 m) long and covering an area of 991,857 square feet (92,243 sq. m)—used highly innovative construction techniques. The building was made entirely of standardized, interchangeable parts, the vast majority of which were mass produced. The iron rods that formed the frame of the building were simply bolted together on site. The construction was highly organized and took only nine months. The palace was specifically designed so that it could be dismantled and reassembled elsewhere, and it was successfully moved to the London suburb of Sydenham in 1852. Tragically, however, it was destroyed by a fire in 1936.

cities to work in factories. This, in turn, meant that cities had to house both large numbers of people and the places where they worked; it was the dawn of the urban world. For all its chaos and complexity, the modern urban world has been made possible by a surprisingly small number of inventions, most notably the use of metal-framed buildings and reinforced concrete.

The age of iron

The Industrial Revolution brought about many dramatic changes, not the least of which was the widespread use of iron in buildings. One of the first demonstrations of this was the iron bridge constructed in 1779 at Coalbrookdale in the county of Shropshire, England. Iron was not only cheaper and stronger than timber or stone, but it could be produced on a large scale. Steel, which was even stronger, was mass produced from 1856 onward, following the invention of the Bessemer converter, named for the English engineer Sir Henry Bessemer (1813–1898).

It wasn't long before iron and steel found their way into buildings. It was used to build the huge Buckingham Palace in London, and soon engineers began to have even bigger ideas.

▼ *The village of Ironbridge, which grew up around the pioneering metal bridge built near the Coalbrookdale mines, is known as the "Birthplace of the Industrial Revolution."*

THE EIFFEL TOWER

The most famous example of an iron-framed structure is the Eiffel Tower, produced for the Paris Exhibition of 1889. It was named for the French engineer Gustave Eiffel (1832–1923), who also designed the gigantic steel framework that supports the Statue of Liberty in New York.

▲ *At 1,063 ft (324 m) tall, the Eiffel Tower was the tallest building in the world until 1930.*

SOCIETY AND INVENTIONS

Ancient skyscrapers

Sana'a, the capital of Yemen, has the oldest apartment buildings in the world. These ancient skyscrapers are 1,400 years old and have several stories, despite being made from clay bricks. Just like in modern cities, landowners had to build upward to make the most of space in the crowded city center.

Balloon framing

By the middle of the 19th century iron-framed construction started to make an impact in the United States, initially in Chicago. It was the second time the city had been at the forefront of building innovation. From around 1830 Chicago had expanded rapidly from a small village thanks to the invention of balloon framing by the American engineer G.W. Snow. This method constructed buildings rapidly around wooden frameworks: long vertical sticks ran from the roof to the floor, and horizontal

▶ *The Flatiron Building was constructed in New York City in 1902, and was one of the first skyscrapers. Its name refers to the building's long, triangular shape.*

boards or joists were nailed to them. Balloon framing cost around half the amount of traditional carpentry and was much faster.

The rise of the skyscraper

Ironically, the very success of balloon framing also led directly to its downfall. In 1871, a fire destroyed many of the balloon-framed buildings in central Chicago. An influential movement of architects, known as the Chicago School, began making buildings with iron frames.

As cities started to grow, the price of land in their centers started to rise, and it became important to make the maximum use of the space available. In theory, a building could always be made taller, but there were two

practical difficulties with this. First, people could not be expected to walk up hundreds of stairs. Second, the weight of the masonry made it impossible to make a building above 16 stories.

The first of these problems was solved in 1854 when American inventor Elisha G. Otis (1811–1861) developed an elevator with an automatic safety device.

The second problem was solved by Chicago engineer William L. Jenney (1832–1907), who developed a strong skeleton of cast-iron columns and beams for his Home Life Insurance Building (completed in 1885). These two inventions removed the height limit on buildings and led directly to that most essential feature of modern cities, the skyscraper.

KEY COMPONENTS

Elevators

In an elevator, the passenger car is hauled up and down by a set of strong steel cables called hoisting ropes. These loop around a pulley wheel, or sheave, which is attached to an electric motor on the roof of the building. The weight of the car is balanced by a counterweight, which considerably reduces the power needed to lift the car.

Early elevators were rickety and dangerous. If the main cable broke, the elevator crashed to the floor. That changed in 1854 when Elisha G. Otis invented an elevator with a safety device. In the Otis elevator, the car traveled between guide rails that had toothed edges. If the cable broke, metal levers sprung outward from the car, locked into the teeth, and stopped the car from falling.

In 1857 Otis's company introduced the world's first ever passenger elevator at the New York china store of E. V. Haughwout. Powered by steam—electric elevators wouldn't arrive for another 25 years—Otis's elevator could transport 6 people at 40 ft (12 m) per minute. Modern-day elevators are capable of traveling at far greater speeds, up to 1,700 ft (510 m) per minute. In fact, they are theoretically capable of moving even more quickly, but it is thought that passengers would find the experience unpleasant.

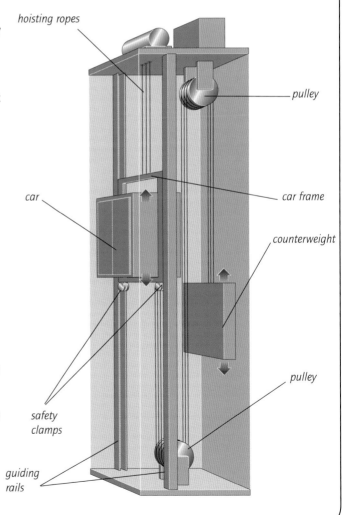

hoisting ropes

pulley

car

car frame

counterweight

pulley

safety clamps

guiding rails

◀ *A 20th-century housing project in Marseille, France, designed by architect Le Corbusier, was constructed using the then-new material of reinforced concrete.*

"MACHINES FOR LIVING IN"

The new structural technologies that emerged in the second half of the 19th century in Chicago and France led to buildings that were increasingly functional. Outside, they were essentially steel skeletons covered with a skin of masonry, concrete, and glass. Inside, they still contained load-bearing walls, which helped support their weight. In other words, the interiors were little different from the buildings of the past.

That changed with the French architect Auguste Perret (1874–1954), who discovered that a building with a strong steel framework no longer needed internal, load-bearing walls. His revolutionary apartment building at 25b rue Franklin, in Paris, did away with the internal walls to produce large areas of open space. It was a forerunner of the open-plan designs that we are familiar with today.

Concrete and steel

For all its innovation, Jenney's first skyscraper still used stone walls. In 1892 French engineer François Hennebique patented reinforced concrete, which was a method of embedding steel bars inside concrete blocks to produce a material much stronger than either concrete or steel alone. Reinforced concrete literally changed the face of architecture and is used in almost every large building and structure today.

What most people regard as typical modern architecture developed at the Bauhaus school of design, which operated from 1919 until 1933 in the German cities of Weimar, Dessau, and Berlin. Under its directors, the German architects Walter Gropius (1883–1969) and Ludwig Mies van der Rohe (1886–1969), this hugely influential school pioneered a stripped-down, highly

▲ *Cleaning the windows on a building clad, or covered, in glass is a big job. Here, window cleaners are using equipment designed for mountaineers to do their job.*

Reinforced concrete

While concrete has existed in some form or other since Roman times, it wasn't until the mid-19th century that the idea of reinforcing it with iron and steel was conceived. The first experiments in reinforced concrete were made by the French gardener Joseph Monier (1823–1906), who in 1867 filed a patent for flowerpots reinforced by an iron cage. Monier's ideas were soon developed by the French builder François Hennebique (1842–1921), who began to use iron bars to strengthen masonry floors.

Hennebique realized that a straight iron bar would not reinforce concrete as efficiently as one that was bent to give support specifically to the areas where it was needed most. Concrete is strong in compression (when squeezed) but weak in tension (when stretched). Figure 1 shows a beam supported by three columns and the areas where the forces of tension and compression are greatest. The straight iron bar in figure 2 strengthens the concrete but doesn't support the areas where the tension is highest. However, changing the shape of the iron bar as shown in figure 3, delivers support to the areas where the concrete is under greatest stress.

▶ The steel reinforcements poke out from a column of concrete. As the metal corrodes inside, the concrete will crack.

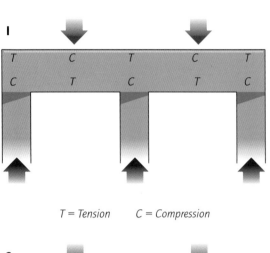

T = Tension   C = Compression

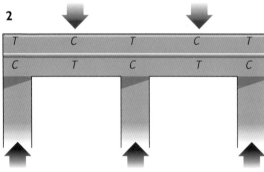

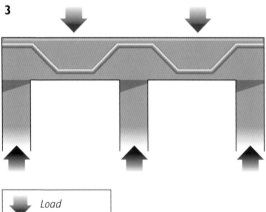

Load

Support

◄ *The Gateway to the West arch in St. Louis has a core of reinforced concrete covered in steel plates.*

functional approach to architecture known as Modernism, which was inspired by a devotion to the power of machines.

The most influential modern architect of the time was the Swissman, Charles-Edouard Jeanneret (1887–1965), who was usually known as Le Corbusier. From 1923, when he published his ideas in the book *Vers une Architecture* (Toward a New Architecture), Le Corbusier was one of the most innovative and controversial figures in his field. Perhaps best known for his statement that a house should be a "machine for living in," he pioneered the concept of mass, low-cost housing.

When people think of Modernist architecture, they usually conjure up pictures of stark grids of concrete, steel, and glass. But the Modernist revolution led to some dazzling

AIR CONDITIONING

In the 20th century, air conditioning became a common feature of buildings. One of the key figures in the development of air conditioning was the American Willis H. Carrier (1876–1950). In 1902, Carrier designed an air-conditioning system that not only circulated cold air throughout the building but also removed humidity from the atmosphere.

Various types of air-conditioning units are in use today, but they all work under the same principles. Incoming air is cleaned, either by fiberglass wool filters or jets of water, before its temperature is adjusted. This is often done by passing it over coils filled with either a refrigerant or hot water, depending on whether the air needs to be heated or cooled. Finally, in order to achieve the desired level of humidity, moisture is either added to or taken away from the air before a system of fans blows it back into the room.

► *A back alley is filled with air-conditioning units, pumping the heat and moisture out of buildings.*

designs around the world. One of the best examples is the Trans World Airlines building at John F. Kennedy International Airport in New York. Completed in 1962 and designed by the Finnish architect Eero Saarinen (1910–1961), its elegantly sweeping wings are a particularly imaginative use of reinforced concrete. Saarinen also designed the Gateway to the West arch in St. Louis, Missouri.

Visionaries and mavericks

One of the most startling and original approaches to the problem of enclosing a space

▲ Modernist buildings are simple boxes that create large living spaces. The windows often make up an entire wall, making it easy to see what is going on outside—and inside.

SOCIETY AND INVENTIONS

Housing the masses

An audacious experiment in social housing by the Swiss architect Le Corbusier, the Unité d'Habitation was built in Marseille, France, between 1946 and 1952. Inside, this block of 337 apartments on 18 floors was like a small town housing 1,800 people. Wide corridors run all the way through, leading to split-level apartments that have their own staircases. The roof of the building includes a garden, swimming pool, and play area for children that includes caves and tunnels. The building also has shops, a school, and an open-air theater.

Le Corbusier's ideas were misinterpreted by other architects trying to recreate his ideas with smaller budgets. Le Corbusier is remembered as the architect whose work led to the badly designed high-rise apartment buildings of the 1960s and 1970s.

◀ High-rise apartment blocks bring people together.

FRANK LLOYD WRIGHT

Although much of modern architecture can be traced back to the gridlike skyscrapers pioneered in Chicago from the 1850s, not all buildings developed along that route. The influential Chicago architect Frank Lloyd Wright (1867–1959) developed his own style of Organic Architecture. By using natural materials, his buildings seem to grow dramatically, but harmoniously, from their environment. With their long horizontal planes close to the ground, they are often instantly recognizable. His most famous building, Fallingwater, a large house built in Pennsylvania in 1937, is constructed above a waterfall.

▼ *The National Congress building in Brasilia has two half spheres. The left dome contains the Senate, while the lower House of Deputies sits in the right, up-turned hemisphere.*

to make a building was proposed by the American architect and engineer Richard Buckminster Fuller (1895–1993). Fuller invented the geodesic dome, a sphere made up of hundreds or thousands of hexagons. Fuller's biggest dome had a diameter of 384 ft (117 m) and was produced for the Union Tank Car Company in Baton Rouge, Florida, in 1958. But he is better known as the designer of America's pavilion at the Expo '67 exhibition in Montreal, Canada: a huge 254-ft (75 m) dome covered by a plastic skin. The space frames used in public exhibition buildings and stadiums work in a similar way to the geodesic dome.

Modern buildings, modern cities

Modern cities are not simply collections of reinforced-concrete skyscrapers. Since the time of the ancient Greeks and Romans, cities have been planned with varying degrees of success.

▲ An atrium runs down the center of a skyscraper hotel. This space provides light but also acts as a chimney for rising warm air. There is often a pool at the base of an atrium to collect rain water.

The evolution of some of the United States' greatest cities has been planned in detail: a plan for Washington, D.C., was worked out as early as 1791. In 1957, a modern new capital city of Brazil was planned. Brasilia, famous for its many unusual buildings, was the work of architect Oscar Niemeyer (born 1907).

Modern ideas about city planning owe as much to environmentalism as to architecture. At the end of the 19th century English visionary Sir Ebenezer Howard (1850–1928) thought up the garden city as a response to the terrible urban conditions created in many cities by the filth of the Industrial Revolution. The garden cities were carefully zoned into business and residential

SCIENTIFIC PRINCIPLES

Geodesic domes and space frames

The weight of the materials in a traditional building, plus the weight of its occupants and contents, must be supported at key points in its structure. The load is supported by the external walls and some of the internal (load-bearing) walls. In a modern skyscraper the load is distributed evenly throughout the building's metal framework. Geodesic domes support the weight of a building or roof by distributing it evenly through a latticework of triangles and hexagons. Each strut in the framework carries the same load. Because there are so many struts, each one bears a relatively small amount of the load and can be made of lightweight material. No intermediate pillars or walls are needed, so these structures are ideal for sports stadiums, museums, and exhibition halls which need large open spaces.

▲ This geodesic dome houses Science World in Vancouver, Canada. It was originally built in 1986.

GREEN HOMES FOR THE FUTURE?

Architects have always been concerned with the way their buildings fit into the environment. But increasing concern for the environment has led to buildings designed specifically to create as little pollution as possible.

Green buildings often get their power from solar panels on the roof or large areas of glass that trap the Sun's heat inside. Sometimes green buildings are designed in a shape that allows air to circulate naturally through the building without the need for air conditioning. Green buildings usually have thick, insulated walls to prevent heat escaping. Other types of green building are designed to blend into their environment. They may be built partly underground or covered with turf. Usually, they are built from wood, stone, or other materials that come from the local area.

▲ *The roof of this eco-friendly house is designed to shade the house, keeping it cool from the Sun. Solar cells on the roof turn the energy in sunlight into electricity to power the house.*

◄ *The city of Tokyo, Japan, now so large that it has joined onto neighboring Yokohama, is the largest city on Earth. It is home to more than 30 million people.*

areas with regions of permanent green belt to give an impression of the countryside. In the 1920s and 1930s these ideas were successfully copied in the U.S. city of Greenbelt, Maryland.

Recognizing that cities have an enormous impact on the environment, planners are designing car-free streets, and public buildings, such as hospitals and schools, are planned to be as close as possible to transportation links.

Yet city planning always seems to be one step behind what people want. High-speed Internet connections have allowed people to work, study, and shop at home and thus avoid the need to commute into a city at all. Just as the Industrial Revolution shaped today's cities, so the technological revolution of the 21st century will shape the cities of the future.

SOCIETY AND INVENTIONS

How cities are planned

Some of the world's oldest cities, such as London, England, have evolved haphazardly out of many small villages and towns. By contrast Paris, France (below), has been built according to a plan, although many of its buildings are now admired for their old-fashioned charm. In most cases, cities contain a mixture of modern planned precincts and older, historic districts.

Planning a city involves a careful consideration of where to place housing, offices, factories, recreation areas, railroads, subway systems, and highways.

Typically, different activities are planned to take place in different areas, or zones.

City plans include making sure there are enough homes, conserving historic buildings, regenerating areas that have become derelict, and ensuring the city and its occupants have a minimum impact on the environment.

▼ *Twelve boulevards in the center of Paris, France, spread out in a star from a central point known as Place L'Etoile—meaning Square of the Star. At the end of the main avenue is La Défense, a district of high-rise office buildings.*

CONTROLLING WATER

Throughout history people have sought new ways of controlling and making use of water more effectively. Over the centuries these efforts have led to some of the largest engineering projects on Earth.

The first major water-supply schemes, going back more than 5,000 years, were used for irrigating crops. For drinking water people would have gone to the nearest clean stream or spring, or used specially dug wells that connected to underground water supplies. The construction of large-scale public supply systems began with the development of cities. Jerusalem, for example, had extensive underground water-storage facilities from around 1000 B.C.

The best known ancient water supply system is that of the Roman Empire, many of whose massive engineering works survive to this day.

▲ Ocean-going cargo ships pass through huge locks in the Panama Canal, a waterway through Central America that connects the Atlantic and Pacific Oceans.

AQUEDUCTS

Aqueducts are long channels that transport water from high natural sources to towns and cities. The first examples were built in Armenia and date back to around 700 B.C. Aqueducts rely on gravity to function and have to slope gradually downward throughout their length. They were thus often forced to take fairly roundabout routes. The Aqua Marcia, which was built in 144 B.C. and supplied water to Rome, stretched 57 miles (91 km), even though the water source was only 23 miles (37 km) away. Every day around 46 million gallons (171 million liters) of water were delivered to the city of Rome in this manner.

▲ The Pont du Gard aqueduct in France is 2,000 years old. It carried 44 million gallons (200 million liters) a day.

To supply the fountains and bathhouses of Rome, many miles of aqueducts were constructed, leading from springs in the hills.

For crossing deep valleys, the Romans (and the Greeks before them) sometimes used inverted siphons—pipes that convey water down a gradient and up the other side. Siphons work if the pipes are strong enough, always full of water, and release the water at a lower level than it originally entered.

Various machines for lifting water were in use in the ancient world, and some can still be found today. They include the *shadoof*, a balanced pole with a counterweight for raising water out of ditches; the *saqiya*, a chain of pots worked by animal power; the Archimedes's screw, a screw-shaped device rotated by hand to lift water; and early forms of pump.

Cleaning up

The Romans' works were not equaled in scale until the 18th and 19th centuries. At that time better water supplies were urgently needed to combat waterborne diseases in the new industrial cities of Europe, as well as to supply industry itself. Gravity-based systems for water distribution were gradually replaced by ones in which steam-powered pumps propelled the water through enclosed water pipes, a transition

INSTANBUL'S WATER WORKS

The Roman city of Constantinople, now Istanbul, Turkey, kept its water in cisterns, an underground storage system. The city has several hundred cisterns, many built in the 6th century by Emperor Justinian. The city's water came from a forest several miles to north and was carried to the cisterns by a series of aqueducts. In 1555, after the city had transferred to Muslim rule, Sultan Suleiman built a new water supply system that channeled spring water to public fountains.

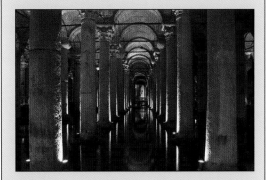

▲ The Basilica Cistern is the largest in Istanbul. Its forest of columns created room for 100,000 tons (90,700 metric tonnes) of water.

that eventually led to the large-scale water supply systems of today.

Rivers and flood control

Many civilizations have grown up around large rivers, yet most rivers inevitably flood from time to time. Sometimes the flood is predictable, as in the annual Nile floods that made ancient Egypt fertile. But unpredictable floods can cause disaster. For some rivers such as the Huang He (Yellow River) in China flood-control measures go back thousands of years. Ways to protect against flooding include deepening and straightening the river channel, building levees (high, reinforced banks), and constructing extra overflow channels in cities.

In the 20th century there were very large schemes to control rivers, including dams to trap floodwater. But rivers are complex systems, and human intervention may have unwanted side effects. A raised bank in one place, for example, may make flooding worse downstream. After the Mississippi River floods of 1993 there was much debate as to whether engineering projects had actually made matters worse by making the river flow faster.

Dams

Dams have been built since ancient times for a variety of reasons, mainly to store water or divert it for irrigation. The earliest dam that we know about was built at Kosheish on the Nile River in Egypt in around 2900 B.C. and was used to supply water to the Egyptian city of Memphis. Unsurprisingly, most of the early

▼ *A town and fields in the Shahdadkot district of southern Pakistan is inundated by flood water from the Indus River in 2010, which damaged many roads and bridges.*

▲ *Lake Powell, one of the largest reservoirs in the world, stretches out behind the Glen Canyon Dam across the Colorado River in Arizona.*

developments in dam design came in the Middle East, with its lack of regular rainfall. The Babylonians (from modern Iraq) and Assyrians built dams from around 700 B.C.

In the last 200 years considerable efforts have been made to use scientific principles to maximize the efficiency of dam design. In the middle of the 19th century engineers such as the Scot William Rankine (1820–1872) began to look at the forces that were exerted on dams and ways that different-shaped dams resisted these forces. One shape that proved to be very effective was the arch. As dam design became more and more scientific, so larger and larger dams could be built. In many cases a hydroelectric plant is built into the dam to harness the power of the river's current.

KEY COMPONENTS

Dams

There are two types of dam: gravity dams and arch dams. Gravity dams are large embankments that rely on their size to withstand the weight of the water behind them. Arch dams are thinner and use their arch shape to transmit the force of the water to the side. They are built of concrete and can only be constructed in narrow gorges, where the surrounding rocks are very strong.

Gravity dams are built of a mixture of earth, rock fragments, or concrete. These dams are often porous and so have a central core of a nonporous clay to hold back the water. A stone lid (known as rip-rap) is built on top to stop erosion from wave action.

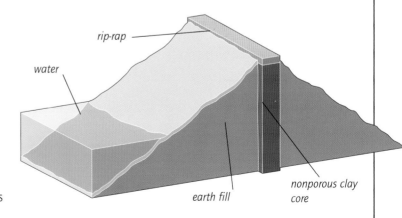

▲ *The largest gravity dams are embankments made of earth or another material taken from the local area.*

Waste and pollution control

Effective means of disposing of domestic sewage came much later in history than water supplies. Although ancient cities such as Mohenjo-Daro (in modern Pakistan) had elaborate drainage systems, in most cases they were aimed mainly at removing surface water. Up until the 19th century human waste was often thrown untreated into the nearest river (as it still is in some places today). The toilets that came into use mainly from the 18th century onward often discharged into pits, or cesspools. The growth of large industrial cities made matters worse. In England in the 1830s cholera epidemics were traced to sewage contaminating public wells.

▲ *Going to the bathroom in Roman times was a social event. Everyone used a communal toilet—there were no cubicles. There was no toilet paper and everyone shared a sponge on a stick.*

WATER PURITY

The purity of water has long been of concern to people. The Romans devised primitive means of telling how pure a particular water source was, and accordingly used water from one source for drinking and another for washing clothes. They also sometimes arranged for sediment to settle out of water before using it.

In many countries, water from a faucet is normally safe for washing and cooking but may require further purification before drinking. Filter jugs (right) are used to take out unwanted minerals and the chemicals used to clean it which can affect its taste.

Some industrial countries then started to construct good sewerage systems. At first, sewerage pipes were connected to the existing drains used for storm water, and human waste passed untreated into nearby rivers. Late in the 19th century sewage-treatment plants were built. The first sewerage plants had tanks to allow suspended material to settle out as sludge before the water was discharged into a river. This is called primary treatment. Modern water works use more elaborate purification systems.

Protecting against the sea

Since ancient times harbors have been provided with outer defenses (breakwaters) to shelter ships at anchor. Modern breakwaters often make

▶ *Plastic litter does not break down naturally and much of it ends up washed out to sea. Ocean currents sweep this pollution into huge "garbage patches."*

SCIENTIFIC PRINCIPLES

Sewage treatment

In a modern urban sewerage plant the sewage goes through two (and often three) separate stages before it is discharged back into a city's rivers and waterways. In the primary treatment stage the sewage is first passed through a filter that removes the largest bits of waste matter. It then flows into a grit chamber, where substances such as sand settle to the bottom of the tank. The sewage then passes into a primary sedimentation tank where fine solids slowly sink to the bottom.

In the second stage the sewage is further purified by exposing it to the natural action of bacteria. One way to do this is to pass compressed air through the sewage (the so-called activated sludge process). Third treatment stages are usually used to address specific types of pollution. For example, the sewage may be subjected to radiation treatment.

▲ *Greasy liquid floats to the surface of sedimentation tanks, where it is skimmed off by booms. Chemicals are added to make smaller particles clump together until they sink as well.*

use of huge interlocking shapes of concrete called tetrapods to absorb the force of the waves. Others are built as vertical walls to reflect rather than absorb the waves' energy.

Engineering may also be applied to the coastline in general. River mouths are most vulnerable, being low-lying and often with large human populations. Storm surges—inrushes of the sea—can cause disastrous flooding.

Global concerns

Early in the 20th century a trend began to build large multipurpose water resource projects, combining irrigation, hydroelectric power, flood control, and other systems to maximize the benefits from a given project. A famous example was the Tennessee Valley Authority

◄ Windmills are used in the Netherlands to pump water out of low-lying areas.

FACTS AND FIGURES

● On average the world's city dwellers consume 80–160 gallons (300–600 liters) of water per person each day. This contrasts with just 5–8 gallons (20–30 liters) per day in rural areas of less-developed countries.

● The amount of water on Earth is fixed and can never be used up. Scientists have estimated this to add up to about 335 million cubic miles (1,400 million cubic km). Around 97 percent of this water is found in the world's oceans.

● At 1,388 million cubic feet (40 million cubic m), the world's largest dam in terms of volume is the Three Gorges Dam in China. The highest is the 1,001-ft (305 m) Jinping I Dam, also in China.

▲ *The Thames Barrier is a rotating dam that can block the Thames River and stop tidal surges flooding London.*

(TVA) scheme of the 1930s. However, climate change and rapid population growth is putting great strain on the world's water resources. Scientists are looking at ever more ingenious ways of managing water. Desalination plants, which take the salt out of sea water, have been used in California and the Middle East since the 1950s but are expensive to run unless cheap energy is available. Probably most important is education—teaching people the importance of conserving water whenever possible.

SOCIETY AND INVENTIONS

The Delta Plan

In 1953 the delta of the Rhine River in the Netherlands was devastated by a major flood. Thousands of people died, and a vast amount of land was ruined by saltwater. The area soon became the subject of a major sea-defense project known as the Delta Plan. Large inlets of the sea were sealed off by dams (right), forming tideless lakes. As people became more aware of environmental issues, however, the original plans were changed. One major dam was replaced by a storm-surge barrier that only operates when the tide is dangerously high. Otherwise the tides ebb and flow as normal. The estuary, which acts as a breeding area for sea fish, has thus been preserved.

▲ *The huge Dutch flood barriers have protected the land, but the coast is eroding away slowly because less silt is being dropped by the river as it empties into the sea.*

BRIDGES AND TUNNELS

Ever since people first began to build roads and paths, bridges and tunnels have allowed them to go over, under, or through obstacles rather than having to travel around them.

A bridge takes a road or walkway, called the deck, over the top of an obstacle such as a river. To do this, it has to have a special structure that will support the weight of the road and anyone on it and distribute the weight toward the points where the bridge meets the ground.

The most basic type of bridge is the beam bridge, formed naturally when a tree falls across a stream. The tree trunk takes the weight of anyone walking across it and distributes it to the banks on either side. The distance between the two supporting banks is known as the span. However, pressure down on the banks causes an

▲ The Golden Gate Bridge across the entrance to San Francisco Harbor was the longest bridge in the world when it opened in 1937. It is the ninth longest today.

opposing force (called a reaction) against it. This makes the trunk bend under the weight of someone standing in the middle and puts the wood under stress—the top of the trunk is being compressed, while the bottom is being stretched. If the tree is not strong enough, it will snap.

This is the basic problem that anyone building a bridge has to deal with, and over thousands of years a number of different solutions have been found.

The girder bridge
The simplest form of bridge is undoubtedly the girder, or beam, bridge. A clapper bridge is specifically a bridge built of stone, but the same

Types of bridge

All bridges are variations on four simple designs—the girder, arch, suspension, and cantilever. These four main types of bridge vary primarily in the way that they bear their load and distribute it to their supports.

In a simple girder bridge (1) the weight is borne by the two supporting pillars and thrusts straight down. As the beam bends under the weight of its load, it is stretched. The material used for a beam bridge therefore has to be able to withstand great tension. For this reason ancient beam bridges made out of stone could have only limited spans.

In order to overcome this, the Romans and other early civilizations began to use arches to build their bridges. In an arched bridge (2) the load exerts a sideways outward force, so arches were firmly buttressed at the side.

In a suspension bridge (3) the deck is held by cables suspended from towers. The weight of the bridge is borne in two ways. Some of the weight pushes downward through the foundations of the towers. However, the vast majority of the weight is held by the cables, which are anchored deep in ground on both sides of the bridge.

The last type of bridge (4) is the cantilever. Here pairs of identically balanced sections are joined by a small central span. Any downward thrust through the pillars is counterbalanced by an equal and opposite upward thrust where the bridge meets the shore.

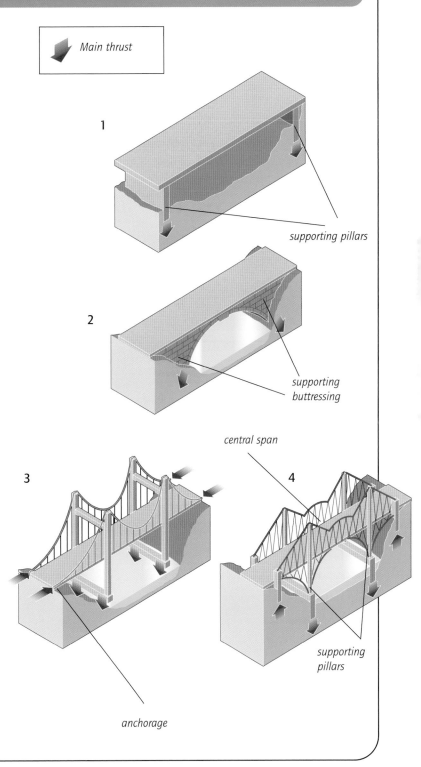

Main thrust

1

supporting pillars

2

supporting buttressing

central span

3

4

supporting pillars

anchorage

CLAPPER BRIDGE

The oldest surviving human-made bridges are variants on the girder bridge known as the clapper bridge. Here piles of flat stones are stacked on top of each other to form supporting piers, while larger, longer stones are laid across the top of them to form the beam. Clapper bridges were built by the Stone Age people of Western Europe as long ago as 2000 B.C. Many examples survive, and some are still in use today.

▲ This 700-year-old clapper bridge was once one of the main routes through Devon in southwestern England. Today, a replacement bridge is used instead—an arch bridge from 1780.

▲ The Rialto Bridge is a 420-year-old arch bridge that crosses the Grand Canal in Venice, Italy. The bridge has a covered walkway lined with shops.

simple method can be used to build wooden bridges. In prehistoric times people built trackways through marshes by hammering wooden piers down into a river bed and then laying beams across them. A slightly more elaborate type of beam bridge has two parallel beams along each edge, with planks laid between them to create a wide deck.

Another advance on the simple girder bridge was the box girder, first used in a bridge by British railroad engineer Robert Stephenson (1803–1859). His Britannia Bridge—a railroad crossing over the Menai Straits in Wales built between 1845 and 1850—consisted of two rectangular wrought iron tubes. The box shape made the tubes extremely strong. Stephenson had planned to give the bridge extra support with suspension cables, but when the final section of girder was in place, he realized that the bridge was strong enough without them.

Arched bridges

Many of the oldest bridges still standing today use arches to support them. The arch works in just the same way as it does in a building,

transferring its own weight and the weight of the deck down and to the sides. Arches avoid the bending forces that can cause beam or girder bridges to break because all the parts are compressed under their own weight. The only way an arch can fall down is if it is allowed to spread to the sides—a series of arches will push against each other where they meet, so this is only a problem at the points where the arches meet the banks (the abutments). Here, the bridge must have solid foundations.

For two thousand years the only arched bridges known in the West used semicircular arches. This was a problem because the deck had to run across the top of the arch, making it very difficult to get a flat deck suitable for horse-drawn vehicles. The answer to this problem is to use a much smaller part of a circle for the

TRUSS BRIDGES

One successful variation on the girder bridge is the truss bridge. A triangular latticework of trusses is put up on either side of the deck. This stiffens the structure and makes it far less likely to break when subjected to heavy loads. The first truss bridge was built by Italian Andreas Palladio (1508–1580) and crossed Italy's Cismon River in 100-ft (33 m) spans.

Properly built, truss bridges are very stable. Most of the bridges that carried the railroad west across the United States had frameworks of wooden trusses, although the first person to properly understand how they worked was the U.S. engineer Squire Whipple (1804-1888) in the 1860s. By this time the truss had been adapted into a number of iron and steel forms. It is still a popular bridge design today.

▲ A train travels across a truss bridge spanning the Volga River in southern Russia.

shape of the arch. The Chinese were building segmental arched bridges as long ago as A.D. 600, but they did not reach the Western world until 1345, when work began on the Ponte Vecchio in Florence, Italy.

The arched bridge has remained popular to the present day. Modern arched bridges are usually built in one piece from steel or reinforced concrete.

Cantilever bridges

The cantilever bridge was another design that originated in Asia. It consists of a long beam extending from a pier that is counterbalanced by another beam on the other side of the pier. The first cantilever bridges were made using planks of wood, each extending slightly farther out over the span. The cantilevers were joined in the middle by a short suspended section. This made the cantilever bridge a very stable design.

In the Western world the cantilever design was popular for railroad bridges, where the cantilever was built from iron or steel and balanced by an identical section extending to

FACTS AND FIGURES

● The bridge with the longest single span in the world is the Akashi Kaikyo Bridge in Japan. The bridge's deck runs for 6,532 ft (1,991 m) between the supporting piles.

● The first suspension bridge to feature steel cables, rather than chains, was the Brooklyn Bridge. It had 1,200 miles (1,931 km) of steel wire, while 100,000 tons (91,000 metric tons) of masonry were needed to secure the cables at their anchorages.

● One of the most ambitious bridge projects of recent years is the Danyang–Kunshan Grand Bridge on the high-speed railroad between Beijing and Shanghai, the two most important cities in China. It opened in 2011. The combined length of the elevated deck is 102.4 miles (164.8 km), and the bridge is just one of 244 (plus 22 tunnels) on the railroad.

▼ The Forth Bridge, was built in 1890 to carry a railroad into Edinburgh, Scotland. It is the world's second longest cantilever bridge after the Quebec Bridge in Canada.

▲ *The high Clifton Suspension Bridge, designed by Isambard Kingdom Brunel and completed in the 1860s, was the location for the world's first bungee jump in 1979.*

meet the land on the opposite side of the pier. Because all the weight was pushed down through the bridge's piers, it was a very good design for carrying heavy vehicles such as trains. The first modern cantilever bridge was built across the Main River in Germany in 1867.

Suspension bridges

Suspension bridges are another very old type of bridge, and again, no one knows who invented them. The oldest known examples are rope bridges from South America and southeast Asia. In these bridges two long ropes are slung across the gap to be bridged and securely fastened onto the land at either end. The deck is hung from these main ropes by shorter, vertical ones.

Suspension bridges did not become popular in the Western world until after the Industrial Revolution. British engineer Thomas Telford (1757–1834) built the first modern suspension bridge across the Menai Straits in Wales in

THE CABLE-STAYED BRIDGE

On first sight, the cable-stayed bridge, with its spectacular arrangement of overhead wires, looks like a suspension bridge. However, it works in a different way and is actually more closely related to girder and cantilever bridges. In a suspension bridge, the cables run freely across the tops of its towers and are only anchored at the ends, where the bridge meets the solid ground. In a cable-stayed bridge, however, the cables are attached directly to the towers, which thus support the bulk of the weight. The first example of such as bridge was Sweden's Strömsund Highway Bridge, opened in 1956.

▲ *The Rama IX Bridge crosses the Chao Phraya River in Bangkok, Thailand.*

1826, using two huge towers to support the main cables. To counter the bridge's weight, the towers had to be anchored to the ground with more cables.

For years suspension bridges were most popular in the U.S. The engineer John Roebling (1806–1869) built a series of bridges using iron and steel cables. Roebling died before his most famous creation, New York's Brooklyn Bridge, could be finished, and the project was completed by his son Washington (1837–1926) in 1866. At this time the Brooklyn Bridge had the longest central span in the world (1,595 ft, or 487 m). Another famous American suspension bridge is the spectacular Golden Gate Bridge of San Francisco. Completed in 1937, the distinctive red bridge features a 4,200-ft (1,280 m) central span.

Tunnels

Tunnels, like bridges, are designed to get around obstacles. But instead of going over them, they go under or through them. Different building methods are used for digging them and holding them up, depending on the type of ground. The ancient Egyptians hollowed out the tombs of their pharaohs using copper saws and reed drills, but this was only possible because Egyptian rock is soft and sandy. Once the cavern had been hollowed out, there was always a danger that the pressure of rock above it would make it collapse, so it was immediately lined with stone blocks. These linings were formed by two uprights piers supporting a horizontal lintel, or beam, which held up the weight of the earth above it.

▲ A high girder bridge carries a highway running out of a tunnel serving Funchal, the capital of the mountainous island of Madeira.

THE FIRST TUNNEL

The earliest known transport tunnel was a foot passageway built under the Euphrates River at Babylon (in modern-day Iraq). Because the riverbed was sandy and waterlogged, it was impossible to tunnel under it, so the river was diverted in the dry season, allowing the tunnel to be built and given a stone lining before the water was allowed back.

SOCIETY AND INVENTIONS

Disasters

Bridge design has developed considerably over the centuries, with bridges becoming increasingly strong and durable and capable of covering longer and longer spans. Sometimes, however, bridge builders have overreached themselves, with disastrous consequences. When it opened in 1940, the Tacoma Narrows Bridge, which crossed Puget Sound in Washington State, was seen as a marvel of modern engineering, the third largest suspension bridge in the world. However, when motorists started to use it, they found it alarmingly unstable, prone to swaying violently from side to side.

On November 7, just four months after it opened, the bridge collapsed in a relatively light wind of 42 mph (68 km/h). When it was reconstructed in 1949, engineers were careful to widen the deck and stiffen it with a series of supporting trusses.

▲ *The collapse of the Tacoma Narrows Bridge was captured on film. No one was hurt in the disaster. Motorists abandoned their vehicles and fled moments before the bridge came crashing down.*

▼ *The towers of Brooklyn Bridge were built of brick and were constructed underwater on the sea bed. Workers went into the water inside pressurized workspaces called caissons.*

▲▶ *Tunnelers dug inside a moveable cage or shield, which protected them from falling rocks and soil. The excavated spoil was carried out behind, while other workers bricked up the tunnel behind the tunnel shield.*

Some of the most impressive early tunnels were built in Persia (modern Iran) around 700 B.C. and were used for irrigation and water supply for towns. These tunnels could be many miles long and were built by digging vertical shafts into the ground and then tunneling along to join them together. The shafts also provided ventilation for the workers.

From the mid-19th century level routes were also needed for railroads. Rail tunneling developed first in Britain and then in the United States, where the construction of the Hoosac Tunnel, linking Upstate New York and Boston, saw the first use of dynamite and steam- and air-powered mechanical drills.

Around the 18th century the Industrial Revolution turned canals into a major transport network, and thousands of miles of new waterway were built in Europe and the U.S. Bridges and tunnels were both very important for the canal network because the waterway had to be built absolutely level over long distances,

ROMAN TUNNELING TECHNIQUES

Even though they had only primitive tools at their disposal, the Romans were still able to construct highly impressive tunnels. One example, linking Naples and Pozzuoli and finished in 36 B.C., stretched for 4,800 ft (1,450 m). Sometimes, when they were tunneling through hard rock, the Romans employed a technique known as fire setting. This involved heating the rock face with fires, and then throwing cold water against it. The sudden cooling cracked the rock, allowing it to be dug out easily. Tunneling through hard rock was more difficult than digging through soft ground but did away with the need for a lining. After the end of the Roman Empire, tunneling methods changed little for over 1,000 years.

to stop the water flowing to one end. The first major canal tunnel was built for the Canal du Midi in France in the 1670s. This was also the first tunnel to use gunpowder charges to blast the rock. Explosives played an extremely important part in tunneling projects from this time on.

WATER TUNNELS

The ancient Greeks and Romans realized that tunnels could be also used for drainage. A tunnel under waterlogged ground would quickly fill with water, draining the land above it so it could be reclaimed for building or farming. They also used tunnels for carrying water supplies.

Tunneling machines

The first tunnel under a major river was finally begun in 1825 by the French engineer Marc Brunel (1769-1849) at the Thames River in London, England. Brunel realized the only way to keep the tunnel from flooding or collapsing was to line it as it was dug. He invented the first excavating machine—a circular framework pushed along the tunnel by hydraulic jacks. The frame was divided into cells, each of which was occupied by a digger. As the diggers excavated the tunnel, workers behind them lined the tunnel with bricks. By the time the framework was pushed forward again, a ring of brickwork

▼ *London's Thames Tunnel, completed in 1842, was originally used by pedestrians and road traffic, before becoming part of the city's subway rail network.*

▶ *A modern tunnel-boring machine has dozens of hard cutting teeth that grind away at the soil and rock as the borer's head spins around.*

was in place to keep the tunnel from collapsing. However, the project was still dangerous—the tunnel flooded several times when diggers hit pockets of water at the face and was not completed until 1843. Another way of building an underwater tunnel is to construct sections of tube on land and then sink them into an underwater trench before filling in the seabed or riverbed on top. This technique was tried even before Brunel invented his tunneling machine, but has only become popular since the 1950s.

Nowadays many major tunnels are constructed using fully automated tunnel-boring

THE CHANNEL TUNNEL

One of the world's most spectacular tunnels is the 30-mile (50 km) long Channel Tunnel (right), which joins Britain and France. After decades in which it had seemed an unrealizable dream, the tunnel finally opened in 1994. It had taken 13,000 workers almost eight years to complete the project, the final cost being approximately $15 billion. Running 130–160 feet (40–50 m) beneath the seabed, the Channel Tunnel is in fact not one tunnel, but three— two main tunnels carrying railroad tracks and a third acting as a service tunnel for road vehicles. It was constructed using huge tunnel-boring machines. During the excavation, they removed eight million cubic yards (six million cubic m) of spoil. The completion of the tunnel has enabled people to travel directly from London to Paris, Brussels, and beyond by high-speed train.

▲ *A journey through the Channel Tunnel by train takes about 20 minutes, at least 70 minutes less than the surface ferry service.*

machines (TBMs). These are often likened to giant mechanical earthworms. At their heads are circular cutting faces that rotate, chipping away at the rock or softer clay face. Behind the cutting heads robot arms line the tunnel with curved panels of concrete as the worm burrows forward. The spoil (waste rock) is taken out to the surface by a series of conveyor belts. The whole machine is guided by a laser system that can detect and correct the slightest deviation from the predetermined path. Major tunnels use two TBMs, which are set to meet in the middle.

KEY COMPONENTS

The Greathead Shield

For centuries the main difficulty facing people attempting to tunnel under rivers was the danger of water flooding the tunnel while it was being constructed. This problem was overcome by Henry Greathead when he invented the Greathead shield, a device that would not be bettered for 75 years. Greathead's machine was similar to earlier devices in that it featured a protective shield that was driven forward by hydraulic jacks. However, Greathead installed a compressed air chamber immediately behind the shield. The air pressure inside was great enough to push against the tunnel face and prevent water from entering the chamber. The miners working in the chamber were thus protected from the dangers of accidental flooding. The compressed air chamber was separated from the rest of the tunnel by a concrete bulkhead. The only ways through were two airlocks, one for the tunnelers and one for the spoil coming out.

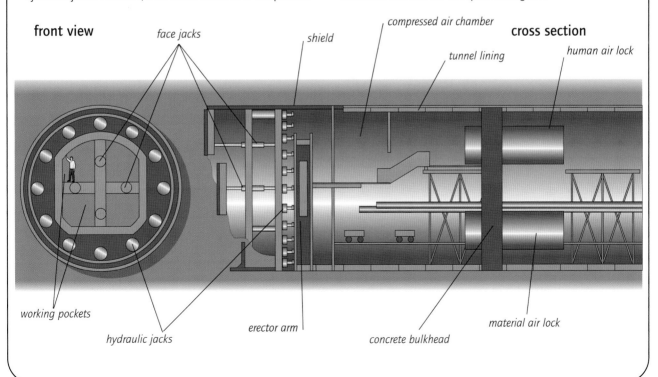

front view

face jacks

shield

compressed air chamber

tunnel lining

cross section

human air lock

working pockets

hydraulic jacks

erector arm

concrete bulkhead

material air lock

THE HOME

The discovery of fire half a million years ago changed the nature of human dwellings. We were now able to cook food and had a new source of light and heat. People have been improving their living conditions ever since.

For thousands of years, the main ways of cooking food were the open fire and an oven built of bricks. Stoves made from pig-iron began to appear in Europe and the U.S. after the Industrial Revolution. They used coal or wood as fuel. However, from the mid-19th century, two new means of cooking would begin to revolutionize the way that people prepared their food—natural gas and electricity.

◀ *Home technology has made housework and cooking easier and faster, and in the modern home, the kitchen and living areas are often together in one large room.*

Cooking with gas and electricity

The first person to use gas to cook food was the German chemist Zachaus Andreas Winzler, who piped gas into the kitchen of his home in Austria in 1802. In 1824, the first gas cooking apparatus went on sale. Designed by Samuel Clegg, it was produced by the Aetna Ironworks in Liverpool, England, and consisted of a small tube, with a number of holes in the side, that could be placed horizontally to fry or vertically to roast food. The first gas stove was designed by the English entrepreneur James Sharp in 1826. It was made commercially available in

FACTS AND FIGURES

● The earliest known cookbook is the *De Re Coquinaria*, published by Apicius in A.D. 62. In it he details the feasts of Emperor Claudius I and his wives Messalina and Agrippina.

● In 1846 the American Nancy Johnson came up with the idea of a freezing machine for making ice creams and sorbets. However, because the idea of women inventing objects was frowned on, Johnson registered the patent in the name of William Young.

● The space shuttle was fitted with a flushing toilet to remove "digestive elimination," as NASA called it. The toilet was flushed by a combination of water and air. It was also equipped with foot restraints and a seat belt.

1834, and in that same year Sharp proved how efficient his stove was with a display of "Gastronomy" cooking, in which a meal for 120 people was prepared. Gas stoves first began to appear in the U.S. in the 1860s. From about the 1870s the metal that stoves were made from began to be covered in a layer of enamel, which made them easier to clean and less likely to rust. In 1923 another step forward was made when the Regulo oven thermostat was introduced. This allowed the cook to set the oven at a specific temperature.

Early examples of electric ovens were shown at an Electric Fair in London in 1891, while in the same year a patent was taken out by the Carpenter Electric Heating Manufacturing

▲ *A cook prepares suet pudding—an old-fashioned dessert made from boiled animal fat.*

FOOD MIXERS AND KITCHEN GADGETS

The business of cutting, shredding, and mixing food can be a long process when done by hand. There have been many attempts to make things quicker in the kitchen. In the 1850s the British company Nye and Lyon introduced the first domestic meat chopper, while in the United States, Enterprise developed machines as diverse as beef shavers, raisin-seeders, and sausage-stuffers. They all relied on hand operation but helped speed up the work of the cook.

One of the first electric machines was invented in 1918 by the U.S. company Landers, Fray, and Clark. It was an electric food mixer that had two small beaters driven by electric motors. The biggest advance in kitchen automation, however, came in 1948 when English inventor Kenneth Wood

designed the Kenwood Chef. It was an all-purpose machine fitted with a large motor that could drive beaters, choppers, squeezers, pasta-makers, and can-openers.

▼ *Blenders are used to make lumpy mixtures into smooth liquids. In recent decades, they have been used to make smoothies, healthy drinks in which fresh fruits are liquidized with juice or milk.*

Company of Minnesota for an electric heating unit made by enameling insulated wires onto cast iron plates. The system was improved by the English engineer R.E.B. Crompton (1845–1940), who used nickel alloys and a double layer of enamel to hold the wires more securely. Among the devices he sold were electric hotplates, as well as frying pans and saucepans that had electric wires embedded in their handles. Cooking with electricity was slow to catch on, since few houses were equipped with electricity until the early 20th century.

In 1924 the Belling company, which had been set up by an electrician who had worked for Crompton 12 years earlier, unveiled the first

◀ *A vintage electric cooker from the early 20th century.*

split-level electric stove, the Modernette. Five years later the company introduced its very popular Baby Belling stove, with three hot rings and an oven beneath. Demand for electric stoves gradually increased after this period as more homes were connected to an electrical supply.

Fridges and freezers

Keeping food fresh has always been difficult. As food gets warm, bacteria on the surface can breed and feed, turning the food moldy or making it rot. One way to keep food from rotting

---

EARLY HOME FURNISHINGS

Some of the oldest surviving examples of furniture are found at Skara Brae on Orkney, off the coast of Scotland. This group of prehistoric stone houses, dating from 500 B.C., was equipped with built-in benches and sleeping areas. More elaborate examples of furniture are found in the pyramid tombs of ancient Egypt. They include elaborately decorated stools, tables, chairs, and beds. The ancient Greeks and Romans were also very skilled furniture makers, developing folding chairs and cupboards and chests. As homes have developed, separate rooms have gained specific uses and with them specific types of furniture and equipment.

▼ *Wealthy Roman people ate lying down on couches. Three couches surrounded a central table. Slaves brought plates of food to the table at the open fourth side.*

DISHWASHERS

In 1827 French engineer Benoit Fourneyron (1802–1867) invented the first practical water turbine, which used flowing water to drive machinery. The principles he used were reversed for the production of the first dishwashers, developed in the United States in the mid-19th century. One such device, invented by Benjamin Howe in 1880, consisted of a frame that held the dishes still while water was hand-cranked around the machine to clean the crockery. A few years later, Josephine Cochrane showed off an improved version at the Chicago World's Fair in 1893. She did not design the machine to save herself washing up. Instead its purpose was to prevent her servants from chipping fine china during cleaning. The first electric dishwasher appeared in 1912. Today's models dry the dishes after cleaning by heating them so they are ready to use straight from the machine.

SCIENTIFIC PRINCIPLES

Cooking with radio waves

In 1945 American scientist Percy LeBaron Spencer (1894–1970) was standing in front of a magnetron, an electronic tube that emits short electromagnetic waves. He noticed that a chocolate bar in his pocket had melted and soon realized that the waves emitted had actually heated the bar. He patented the first microwave oven in 1945. The first home ovens appeared in 1965.

When a microwave oven is turned on, the food inside is bombarded by high-frequency electromagnetic waves. The waves cause water molecules inside the food to vibrate, raising its temperature and thus cooking it. A microwave oven cooks food in a fraction of the time that a conventional oven takes.

However, microwave ovens do have their drawbacks. For example, despite recent developments, they are still unable to brown or crisp foods like a normal oven, so although food is made piping hot, it does do not look or taste quite right.

◄ An ice-making machine from the 1860s used the act of compression and rapid expansion of ammonia gas to draw heat out of water, turning it into ice.

Industrial refrigeration techniques were first developed in the 19th century to enable ships to carry meat and other perishables on long journeys from Europe across the Atlantic. In 1876 the German engineer Karl von Linde (1834–1934) designed the first domestic refrigerator. It used ammonia as a refrigerant, which was pumped around using a small steam pump.

In 1913 the Domelre (Domestic Electric Refrigerator) Company unveiled its first household refrigerator in Chicago. It proved a success, and further developments were made by U.S. inventor Nathaniel Wales, whose

is to keep it cool. Early larders had shelves made of materials like slate and marble that helped maintain a cooler atmosphere. In the late 19th century the first insulated ice-chests began to appear. These were usually lined with either zinc or slate. Ice was put inside the chest, and the food was placed on top.

DOING THE LAUNDRY

For centuries, people have washed their clothes by hand in streams. Away from natural water supplies, clothes were simply washed in wooden or iron tubs. Often a rod or paddle known as a dolly was used to squash and stir the clothes. This system was mechanized in 1858 by the U.S. inventor Hamilton Smith.

The first electric washing machine was invented in 1907 by Alva J. Fisher. A small motor was used to rotate the dolly. This design was improved in 1924, when a combined electric washer–spin drier was produced by the Savage Arms corporation of New York. However, it was a very cumbersome machine to operate. After washing, the drum—still full of wet clothes—had to be lifted and placed on another drive shaft. It was not until the 1950s that the easy-to-use automatic machines finally appeared.

▲ Dobi wallas, Indian laundrymen, clean clothes in open-air tanks. The clean clothes are then delivered to their owners.

Kelvinator was first sold in 1916. The Frigidaire appeared one year later. Many of these early refrigerators were noisy because of the electric motors they used. However, in 1922 the Swedes

Carl Munster and Balzar von Platen built the first silent and functional refrigerator. This was mass produced by the Electrolux company of Sweden in 1925.

SCIENTIFIC PRINCIPLES

How a refrigerator works

Like all refrigeration systems, domestic electric refrigerators make use of the way gases behave when they expand quickly. Adding heat to a gas makes it expand, but a refrigerator makes a liquid, called a refrigerant, evaporate (become gas) and expand without adding heat. The expanding gas then takes heat from the surroundings, making that colder.

The refrigerator contains three main elements—an evaporator, a compressor, and a condenser. The refrigeration cycle begins when the refrigerant is pushed along a pipe and through a nozzle. This lowers the pressure of the refrigerant, turning it into a gas as it enters the evaporator. As the refrigerant vaporizes, it absorbs heat from the air inside the fridge, lowering the temperature. The cold gaseous refrigerant continues to travel around the maze of pipes that make up the evaporator until it reaches the compressor. The compressor is used to push the refrigerant into and out of the condenser. This increases the pressure on the gas, condensing it back into a liquid. As it does so, it gives out the heat it absorbed, which escapes out of the back of the refrigerator into the room at large. The cycle then begins again.

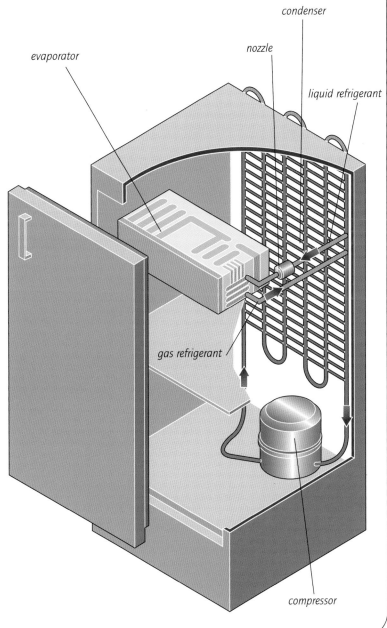

condenser

nozzle

liquid refrigerant

evaporator

gas refrigerant

compressor

Bathrooms

Baths of one form or another have existed for thousands of years. Early examples have been found in the Indus Valley, in modern-day Pakistan, that date back to 2500 B.C. However, despite this, the bathroom has only become a commonplace part of the home in comparatively recent years. In Europe, for example, the bathroom practically disappeared after the fall of the Roman Empire and did not reappear in most houses until the late 19th century.

It was then that systems were developed in which water was heated in a central boiler. One of the first of these was the Ewart Califont. Developed in 1899, it supplied hot water to

◀ This old bath tub was carved from a solid piece of marble.

every tap in the house from a boiler in the basement.

Bathtubs themselves were originally made of iron. However, as they got older, they started to rust. The solution to this problem was to coat the iron in porcelain enamel. The first lightweight, enameled bathtubs were put in Pullman railroad coaches in 1900.

IN HOT WATER

The biggest obstacle to taking a regular bath was getting enough hot water. The simplest way to do this was to heat water in the kitchen and then carry it to wherever the bathtub was located. In order to overcome this inconvenience, in 1827 the Thompson company produced a bath that contained its own heater. Water passed from a storage tank into a cylinder furnace and then into the bath. In 1868 Benjamin Maugham invented the geyser for heating water for baths. In it a tube carrying water spiraled through a cylinder that contained gas burners.

Toilets

The first attempts to mechanize the toilet came in 1596, when a water closet designed by the English courtier Sir John Harrington (1561–1612) was installed at Richmond Palace in London. Harrington's water closet had a seat over a bowl and a pipe to let water in to clean away the contents. Only two Harrington toilets were ever installed, and for 200 years nothing further was heard of the flush system. Then, in 1775 the English watchmaker Alexander Cummings patented the valve closet. It had two valves, one to let the water in and another that controlled the outlet at the bottom of the pan. Cummings's closet was modified by English cabinet maker Joseph Bramah (1748–1814) and remained popular until the end of the 19th century.

These early toilets were made out of metal. However, in 1870 the British potter Thomas Twyford made the first all-ceramic WC. It was Twyford who added the familiar S-bend outlet pipe, which provided a water-seal that kept out smells from the drains. The system was further modified in 1889 when a British plumber named Davis Bostel invented the so-called washdown flush mechanism, a system that is still in widespread use today.

▶ *Before homes were fitted with running water and indoor bathrooms, people washed in their bedrooms using water poured from a jug into a large bowl, or basin.*

SOCIETY AND INVENTIONS

Bathing

Public attitudes to bathing have fluctuated wildly over the centuries and have varied considerably from culture to culture. For many ancient civilizations bathing was a religious imperative. The importance of cleanliness to the Hindu lifestyle explains the existence of 4,500-year-old public baths in the Indus Valley in modern-day Pakistan. Ancient Rome was another place where bathing was common. Although few private houses had bathrooms, public baths were numerous and could hold as many as 1,600 people at a time. However, in Europe in the Middle Ages the practice of bathing declined drastically. In some countries even the wealthy did not bathe. For example, the 16th-century royal palace at Versailles, France, despite having elaborate fountains, did not have any bathrooms at all. The rich just used perfume to hide any bad smells. Bathing came back into fashion in Europe in the late 19th century. Today, attitudes vary widely from country to country. While in the Western world people use baths primarily to get clean, in Japan people are expected to wash before they get into the bath, which is used for relaxation.

▲ *The English city of Bath is named for its large Roman baths, which are fed by a naturally hot spring.*

Housework

American Hiram H. Herrick patented a carpet sweeper in 1858. This device was improved in 1876 by Melville R. Bissell (1843–1889), the owner of a porcelain shop, who was allergic to the dust from the straw used to pack his pots. He developed a broom equipped with a cylindrical brush that pushed the dust into a container.

In 1901, the English civil engineer Hubert Cecil Booth designed the first vacuum cleaner. Booth had seen presentation cleaning machines that

◀ In the 19th century, chimney sweeps were regular visitors to a house, clearing the soot from chimneys with long, flexible brooms.

blew dust from the carpet. Booth realized that dirt could be collected more effectively by suction. Booth's British Vacuum Cleaning Company used large horse-drawn vacuum cleaners that traveled from house to house and were operated by a team of uniformed employees. Booth's machine was very cumbersome—it was powered by a heavy gas motor, while its suction hoses were 100 ft (30 m) long. These problems were overcome in 1907, when the U.S. inventor Murray Spengler developed a much lighter machine that was powered by a small electric fan. However, Spengler was unable to market his invention and sold the rights to a leather manufacturer by the name of William Hoover (1849–1932). The Hoover Model "O" was launched the following year and proved to be an immediate success.

BOSTEL'S TOILET

The design of the washdown toilet (below), originally the work of British plumber David Bostel, has been remarkably enduring. In Bostel's system an overhead cistern supplies the water that flushes the toilet bowl. When a chain or handle is pulled, a plunger is raised within a syphon unit. Water is then pushed through an inverted U-bend and down into the bowl, washing away the contents. When this happens, the water level inside the cistern drops, until a float, called the ball cock, falls to a certain level opening an inlet valve. As the water rises, so does the ball cock, which closes the valve when the cistern has refilled for the next flush.

▲ Litter is swept from city streets today by trucks equipped with rotary brooms and powerful vacuum cleaners.

Vacuum cleaners

In a modern upright vacuum cleaner a rotating spiral brush driven by a rubber belt beats the carpet as it runs over it. This loosens any dirt or dust that is stuck to the carpet fibers. At the same time, an electric fan rotates inside the vacuum cleaner. The fan creates a partial vacuum that pulls air up through a vertical tube connected to a disposable bag. As the air is sucked up the tube, it pulls with it any dirt or dust that has been loosened by the rotating brush. The mixture of air and dust is sucked into the bag. However, while the air passes straight through the bag and out the back of the cleaner, the dust and dirt become trapped and build up at the bottom of the sack. Once the bag is full, it is simply taken out and replaced.

Another popular type of vacuum cleaner is the canister cleaner. It features a nozzle at the end of a long tube connected to flexible hose. The canister cleaner functions in a similar way to an upright model. However, because it does not have a brush beating the carpet, the canisters cleaner relies entirely on the vacuum to remove the dirt and thus needs a more powerful motor.

Bagless cleaners suck up dirt in a spinning vortex of air. As the air spins inside the cleaner, the heavy dust and dirt particles are pushed to the side by centrifugal force and they settle inside a bin, while the clean air continues upward and out of the machine through a filter that removes the finest dust. When the bin is full, it is detached from the machine, emptied, and then reattached for use again.

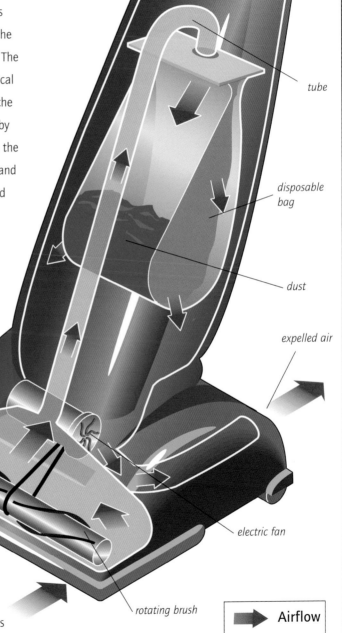

tube

disposable bag

dust

expelled air

electric fan

rotating brush

| Airflow |

1,800,000 B.C. The earliest tools yet discovered are made around this time in the Olduvai Gorge, Tanzania, for cutting meat.

600,000–500,000 B.C. Humans discover fire.

30,000 B.C. The first baked clay objects are made.

10,000 B.C. The first clay pots are made.

4000 B.C. Glazes are used to make pottery watertight.

2900 B.C. Earliest dam is built on the Nile River in Egypt.

2700s B.C. Early stone buildings date from this period.

2560 B.C. The Great Pyramid of Giza is built over a period of about 15 years. The pyramid is the tallest building in the world for more than 3,000 years, until Lincoln Cathedral is built taller in A.D. 1311.

1500 B.C. Iron smelting is first carried out on a large scale.

1000 B.C. Underground water-storage facilities are built in Jerusalem.

600 B.C. Chinese develop the blast furnace to make iron.

A.D. 62 The earliest known cookbook is published.

800 The Chinese produce porcelain, a strong but light form of china.

1494 Monk John Cor distills whiskey for his abbey.

1712 Thomas Newcomen develops a steam engine for removing water from mines.

1779 The first iron bridge in the Western world is constructed near the Coalbrookdale mine fields in England.

1784 Henry Cort patents the puddling process for making wrought iron.

1794 Jacob Schweppe introduces the fizzy drink after Joseph Priestly discovers in 1770 that carbon dioxide dissolved in water creates a refreshing drink.

1795 Nicolas Appert develops a new canning system of preserving food by heating it in sealed containers.

1801 Joseph-Marie Jacquard devises an automatic loom.

1824 Portland cement is patented by Joseph Aspdin.

1826 The gas stove is designed by James Sharp. Thomas Telford builds the first modern suspension bridge.

1844 John Gorrie builds a refrigerator.

1850s Oscar Levi Strauss invents modern jeans. Amelia Bloomer invents bloomers—pants for women.

1854 Elisha G. Otis develops a safe elevator.

1856 Henry Bessemer invents the Bessemer converter for making steel cheaply.

1867 The first modern cantilever bridge is built.

1869 Margarine is invented by Hippolyte Megè-Mouriès as an alternative to butter.

1876 Alexander Graham Bell and Elisha Gray independently file patents for telephones. Karl von Linde designs the first domestic refrigerator.

1882 The first hydroelectric power plant is built at Appleton, Wisconsin.

1883–1885 The first skyscraper is constructed in Chicago.

1892 François Hennebique patents reinforced concrete.

1901 Hubert Cecil Booth designs the first vacuum cleaner.

1907 Alva J. Fisher invents an electric washing machine.

1915 C. Sullivan and W. C. Taylor create a type of heat-resistant glass called Pyrex.

1924 Clarence Birdseye's company is making frozen food.

1935 Wallace Hume Carothers invents nylon.

1988 The Seikan Tunnel under the Tsugaru Strait connecting Japan's Honshu and Hokkaido islands is the longest rail tunnel in the world at 33.5 miles (53.9 km).

2009 Burj Khalifa in Dubai is completed, reaching more than half a mile into the sky. The building had become the world's tallest

structure in 2008 when it was still several months from completion.

2011 Danyang-Kunshan Grand Bridge opens on the high-speed railroad between Beijing and Shanghai. The bridge is more than 100 miles (160 km) long and carries the track over rugged hills and a 5.6 mile (9 km) section across a lake.

GLOSSARY

ancestors The people who came before those people alive today.

ancient Greece A civilization that existed on the mainland and islands of modern-day Greece and Turkey between 2000 and 300 B.C.

architect A person who designs buildings. The word comes from the Greek words for "chief builder."

atrium An open space inside a building.

buttress A structure usually made from brick or stone that is built against a wall to support and reinforce it.

cement A fine powder that is added to sand and water to make concrete. As the mixture dries the cement binds the sand together into a solid rock-like substance. Cement is made by heating limestone rocks. The first cements were naturally heated volcanic ashes.

centrifugal Relating to a force that seems to pull a thing outward as it rotates around an axis.

cistern A water storage tank, often buried underground to keep it cool.

composite A material that is made up of a mixture of other substances. The overall material takes on the characteristics of its ingredients. Composite materials include plastics and wattle and daub.

compression The act of being made more compact by the application of force.

corrode When a substance reacts with the water and salts in the surroundings, becoming weaker and disintegrating. Rust is the result of iron corroding.

deck The horizontal section of a bridge that carries the road, rail track, or walkway.

engineering Using scientific knowledge to solve problems and construct machines, buildings, and structures suited for a particular job.

foundations The place where a building meets the ground. Foundations in soft ground must be buried deeply to provide enough support.

gravity A natural force that attracts two masses toward one another. Among its many effects, gravity draws objects toward Earth's surface and keeps the planets in orbit around the Sun.

Industrial Revolution A great change in social and economic organization brought about by the replacement of hand tools by machines and power tools, and the development of large-scale industrial production methods. The Industrial Revolution started in England around 1760 and spread to the rest of Europe and the United States.

keystone The stone at the top of an arch where the opposite curves meet.

lock A gated section on a canal or river that allows craft to travel up and down steep gradients.

medieval Of or from the Middle Ages.

microwave An electromagnetic wave with a wavelength between 1 mm and 300 mm. Microwaves are used for radar, communications, and heating foods. They are a type of radio wave, used in telecommunications, but have a shorter wavelength—hence the name microwave.

Middle Ages A period of European history that ran from around A.D. 500 to about 1450.

migration When people or animals move in search of a new place to live, better suited to their needs.

mortar A sticky paste that is used to glue bricks and stones together. Basic mortar contains mud and clay, but later forms also include cement.

mosque A Muslim place of worship often characterized by a tall tower, called a minaret, from which the faithful are called to prayer.

nomads People who, instead of having a fixed home, travel from place to place in search of fresh pastures and water for themselves and their animals.

pollution Adding a large amount of unwanted materials into the air, soil, lakes, or oceans. Natural processes cannot always remove or absorb this extra material, which may build up, causing a range of problems.

porous When a solid is full of small holes through which liquids can pass. Many rocks are porous, so water can flow through them.

pressurized To have air packed into it to above the levels of the atmosphere.

radiation The act of giving off radioactive particles, heat, or electromagnetic waves.

refrigerant A fluid used to transfer heat from one space to another. The refrigerant is usually pumped around a closed circuit, absorbing heat from the cooler space and releasing it in the warmer space.

reservoir an artificial lake that is created behind a dam.

Rome The ancient civilization that began in the Italian city of Rome around 700 B.C. and had established a vast empire around the Mediterranean Sea by 200 A.D. The Romans are noted for being the first to bring law and order to Europe and for their great works of engineering.

solar panels Collections of solar cells used to convert sunlight into electrical energy. They are often used to provide electricity on spacecraft.

sphere A circular solid. A globe or ball is a sphere. Half a sphere is known as a hemisphere.

strait A narrow seaway.

suspend To hang.

tension A force that opposes attempts to deform an object. A piece of elastic being stretched is under tension.

vacuum When all the air has been sucked out of an area, leaving nothing behind.

vortex A flow or air of water in a spiral. Whirlpools and tornadoes are natural vortices.

voussoir A curved stone used to create an arch.

waterlogged A porous solid that is filled with water.

ziggurat A tall raised platform built in Mesopotamia—the ancient land around the Euphrates and Tigris Rivers in modern-day Turkey, Syria, Iraq, and Iran.

FURTHER RESEARCH

Books

Bridge Building: Bridge Designs and How They Work by Diana Briscoe. Bloomington, MN: Red Brick Learning, 2005.

Construction: Building the Impossible by Nathan Aaseng. Minneapolis: Oliver Press, 2000.

Steven Caney's Ultimate Building Book by Steven Caney. Philadelphia: Running Press Kids, 2006.

Thinking Big: America's Greatest Constructions by Elaine Pascoe. San Diego: Thomson Gale, 2004.

Toilets, Toasters & Telephones: The How and Why of Everyday Objects by Susan Goldman Rubin. San Diego: Harcourt, Inc., 1998.

Websites

Building Big
http://www.pbs.org/wgbh/buildingbig/index.html

Compare Burj Khalifa with Other Skyscrapers
http://www.burjkhalifa.ae/the-tower/worlds-tallest-towers.aspx

What If Hoover Dam Broke?
http://science.howstuffworks.com/engineering/structural/hoover-dam-broke.htm

INDEX